STARTUP VC – GUIDE

EVERYTHING ENTREPRENEURS NEED TO KNOW ABOUT VENTURE CAPITAL AND STARTUP FUNDRAISING

JASON THIEL

Copyright © Jason Thiel
All Rights Reserved.

ISBN 978-1-63920-943-9

This book has been published with all efforts taken to make the material error-free after the consent of the author. However, the author and the publisher do not assume and hereby disclaim any liability to any party for any loss, damage, or disruption caused by errors or omissions, whether such errors or omissions result from negligence, accident, or any other cause.

While every effort has been made to avoid any mistake or omission, this publication is being sold on the condition and understanding that neither the author nor the publishers or printers would be liable in any manner to any person by reason of any mistake or omission in this publication or for any action taken or omitted to be taken or advice rendered or accepted on the basis of this work. For any defect in printing or binding the publishers will be liable only to replace the defective copy by another copy of this work then available.

Contents

1. Venture Capital	1
2. What Is Venture Capital	3
3. Venture Capital Company	15
4. Finding A Venture Capital Company	20
5. Obtaining Venture Capital	23
6. Financing Tips	25
7. Attracting Vc	28
8. Four Steps	30
9. How To Rise Vc	33
10. Elements Of A Term-sheet	39
11. Rejecting Reasons	44
Disclaimer	47

ONE
VENTURE CAPITAL

Venture capital represents financial investment in a highly risky proposition in the hope of earning a high rate of return. While the concept of venture capital is perhaps as old as the human race, the practice of venture capitalism has remained somewhat fragmented and individualized through its long history. Only in the last four decades or so has the field of venture capital acquired a certain coalescence, maturity and sophistication, particularly in the US.

The origin of venture capital in its modern form may be traced to General Doriot, who established the American Research and Development Fund at the Massachusetts Institute of Technology in 1946, to finance the commercial exploitation of new technologies developed in US universities. The small business act of the US permitted the Small Business Administration to license and even support financially small business investment companies engaged in venture capital finance, provided fuel to the growth of venture capital finance.

Larger companies in the US like Xerox, 3M and General Electric entered the field with their venture capital divisions. These examples from the US stimulated the development of venture capital throughout the world. Though the initial efforts made in the early seventies to introduce venture capital were rather unsuccessful, the changed environment of the eighties witnessed a phenomenal growth of hi-tech industries and provided a fertile ground for the blossoming of venture capital.

Venture capital plays a helping hand in the financing of startup and early stage businesses, as well as businesses in ""turn around"" situations. Firms raise funds from different sources. Some funds like share capital are kept permanently in the business. Some funds like debentures are kept for long periods; while some funds are kept for short periods. The entire composition of these funds in an organization is generally termed a financial structure. Generally, the short-term funds are excluded since they are shifting often and the composition of long-term funds is known as capital structure.

TWO
WHAT IS VENTURE CAPITAL

Venture capital is money provided by professionals who invest alongside management in young, rapidly growing companies that have the potential to develop into significant economic contributors. Venture capital is an important source of equity for start-up companies.

Professionally managed venture capital firms generally are private partnerships or closely-held corporations funded by private and public pension funds, endowment funds, foundations, corporations, wealthy individuals, foreign investors, and the venture capitalists themselves.

Venture capitalists generally:

- Finance new and rapidly growing companies;
- Purchase e?uity securities;
- Assist in the development of new products or services;
- Add value to the company through active participation;
- Take higher risks with the expectation of higher rewards;
- Have a long-term orientation

When considering an investment, venture capitalists carefully screen the technical and business merits of the proposed company. Venture capitalists only invest in a small percentage of the businesses they review and have a long-term perspective. Going forward, they actively work with the company's management by contributing their experience and business savvy gained from helping other companies with similar growth challenges.

Venture capitalists mitigate the risk of venture investing by developing a portfolio of young companies in a single venture fund. Many times they will co-invest with other professional venture capital firms. In addition, many venture partnership will manage multiple funds simultaneously. For decades, venture capitalists have nurtured the growth of America's high technology and entrepreneurial communities resulting in significant job creation, economic growth and international competitiveness. Companies such as Digital Equipment Corporation, Apple, Federal Express, Compa?, Sun Microsystems, Intel, Microsoft and Genentech are famous examples of companies that received venture capital early in their development.

Private E?uity Investing

Venture capital investing has grown from a small investment pool in the 1960s and early 1970s to a mainstream asset class that is a viable and significant part of the institutional and corporate investment portfolio. Recently, some investors have been referring to venture investing and buyout investing as "private e?uity investing." This term can be confusing because some in the investment industry use the term "private e?uity" to refer only to buyout fund investing.

In any case, an institutional investor will allocate 2% to 3% of their institutional portfolio for investment in alternative assets such as private equity or venture capital as part of their overall asset allocation. Currently, over 50% of investments in venture capital/private equity comes from institutional public and private pension funds, with the balance coming from endowments, foundations, insurance companies, banks, individuals and other entities who seek to diversify their portfolio with this investment class.

What is a Venture Capitalist?

The typical person-on-the-street depiction of a venture capitalist is that of a wealthy financier who wants to fund start-up companies. The perception is that a person who develops a brand new change-the-world invention needs capital; thus, if they can't get capital from a bank or from their own pockets, they enlist the help of a venture capitalist.

In truth, venture capital and private equity firms are pools of capital, typically organized as a limited partnership, that invests in companies that represent the opportunity for a high rate of return within five to seven years. The venture capitalist may look at several hundred investment opportunities before investing in only a few selected companies with favorable investment opportunities. Far from being simply passive financiers, venture capitalists foster growth in companies through their involvement in the management, strategic marketing and planning of their investee companies. They are entrepreneurs first and financiers second.

Even individuals may be venture capitalists. In the early days of venture capital investment, in the 1950s and 1960s, individual investors were the archetypal venture investor. While this type of individual investment did not totally disappear, the modern venture firm emerged as the dominant venture investment vehicle. However, in the last few years, individuals have again become a potent and increasingly larger part of the early stage start-up venture life cycle. These "angel investors" will mentor a company and provide needed capital and expertise to help develop companies. Angel investors may either be wealthy people with management expertise or retired business men and women who seek the opportunity for first-hand business development.

Investment Focus

Venture capitalists may be generalist or specialist investors depending on their investment strategy. Venture capitalists can be generalists, investing in various industry sectors, or various geographic locations, or various stages of a company's life. Alternatively, they may be specialists in one or two industry sectors, or may seek to invest in only a localized geographic area.

Not all venture capitalists invest in "start-ups." While venture firms will invest in companies that are in their initial start-up modes, venture capitalists will also invest in companies at various stages of the business life cycle. A venture capitalist may invest before there is a real product or company organized (so called "seed investing"), or may provide capital to start up a company in its first or second stages of development known as "early stage investing." Also, the venture capitalist may provide needed financing to help a company grow beyond a critical mass to become more successful ("expansion stage financing").

The venture capitalist may invest in a company throughout the company's life cycle and therefore some funds focus on later stage investing by providing financing to help the company grow to a critical mass to attract public financing through a stock offering. Alternatively, the venture capitalist may help the company attract a merger or acquisition with another company by providing liquidity and exit for the company's founders.

At the other end of the spectrum, some venture funds specialize in the acquisition, turnaround or recapitalization of public and private companies that represent favorable investment opportunities.

There are venture funds that will be broadly diversified and will invest in companies in various industry sectors as diverse as semiconductors, software, retailing and restaurants and others that may be specialists in only one technology.

While high technology investment makes up most of the venture investing in the U.S., and the venture industry gets a lot of attention for its high technology investments, venture capitalists also invest in companies such as construction, industrial products, business services, etc. There are several firms that have specialized in retail company investment and others that have a focus in investing only in "socially responsible" start-up endeavors.

Venture firms come in various sizes from small seed specialist firms of only a few million dollars under management to firms with over a billion dollars in invested capital around the world. The common denominator in all of these types of venture investing is that the venture capitalist is not a passive investor, but has an active and vested interest in guiding, leading and growing the companies they have invested in. They seek to add value through their experience in investing in tens and hundreds of companies.

Some venture firms are successful by creating synergies between the various companies they have invested in; for example one company that has a great software product, but does not have adequate distribution technology may be paired with another company or its management in the venture portfolio that has better distribution technology.

Length of Investment

Venture capitalists will help companies grow, but they eventually seek to exit the investment in three to seven years. An early stage investment make take seven to ten years to mature, while a later stage investment many only take a few years, so the appetite for the investment life cycle must be congruent with the limited partnerships' appetite for liquidity. The venture investment is neither a short term nor a liquid investment, but an investment that must be made with careful diligence and expertise.

Corporate Venturing

One form of investing that was popular in the 1980s and is again very popular is corporate venturing. This is usually called "direct investing" in portfolio companies by venture capital programs or subsidiaries of nonfinancial corporations. These investment vehicles seek to find qualified investment opportunities that are congruent with the parent company's strategic technology or that provide synergy or cost savings.

These corporate venturing programs may be loosely organized programs affiliated with existing business development programs or may be self-contained entities with a strategic charter and mission to make investments congruent with the parent's strategic mission. There are some venture firms that specialize in advising, consulting and managing a corporation's venturing program.

The typical distinction between corporate venturing and other types of venture investment vehicles is that corporate venturing is usually performed with corporate strategic objectives in mind while other venture investment vehicles typically have investment return or financial objectives as their primary goal. This may be a generalization as corporate venture programs are not immune to financial considerations, but the distinction can be made.

The other distinction of corporate venture programs is that they usually invest their parent's capital while other venture investment vehicles invest outside investors' capital.

Commitments and Fund Raising

The process that venture firms go through in seeking investment commitments from investors is typically called "fund raising." This should not be confused with the actual investment in investee or "portfolio" companies by the venture capital firms, which is also sometimes called "fund raising" in some circles. The commitments of capital are raised from the investors during the formation of the fund. A venture firm will set out prospecting for investors with a target fund size. It will distribute a prospectus to potential investors and may take from several weeks to several months to raise the requisite capital. The fund will seek commitments of capital from institutional investors, endowments, foundations and individuals who seek to invest part of their portfolio in opportunities with a higher risk factor and commensurate opportunity for higher returns.

Because of the risk, length of investment and illiquidity involved in venture investing, and because the minimum commitment re?uirements are so high, venture capital fund investing is generally out of reach for the average individual. The venture fund will have from a few to almost 100 limited partners depending on the target size of the fund. Once the firm has raised enough commitments, it will start making investments in portfolio companies.

Capital Calls

Making investments in portfolio companies requires the venture firm to start "calling" its limited partners commitments. The firm will collect or "call" the needed investment capital from the limited partner in a series of tranches commonly known as "capital calls". These capital calls from the limited partners to the venture fund are sometimes called "takedowns" or "paid-in capital." Some years ago, the venture firm would "call" this capital down in three e?ual installments over a three year period. More recently, venture firms have synchronized their funding cycles and call their capital on an as-needed basis for investment.

Illiquidity

Limited partners make these investments in venture funds knowing that the investment will be long-term. It may take several years before the first investments starts to return proceeds; in many cases the invested capital may be tied up in an investment for seven to ten years. Limited partners understand that this illiquidity must be factored into their investment decision.

Other Types of Funds

Since venture firms are private firms, there is typically no way to exit before the partnership totally matures or expires. In recent years, a new form of venture firm has evolved: so-called "secondary" partnerships that specialize in purchasing the portfolios of investee company investments of an existing venture firm. This type of partnership provides some liquidity for the original investors. These secondary partnerships, expecting a large return, invest in what they consider to be undervalued companies.

Advisors and Fund of Funds

Evaluating which funds to invest in is akin to choosing a good stock manager or mutual fund, except the decision to invest is a long-term commitment. This investment decision takes considerable investment knowledge and time on the part of the limited partner investor. The larger institutions have investments in excess of 100 different venture capital and buyout funds and continually invest in new funds as they are formed.

Some limited partner investors may have neither the resources nor the expertise to manage and invest in many funds and thus, may seek to delegate this decision to an investment advisor or so-called "gatekeeper". This advisor will pool the assets of its various clients and invest these proceeds as a limited partner into a venture or buyout fund currently raising capital. Alternatively, an investor may invest in a "fund of funds," which is a partnership organized to invest in other partnerships, thus providing the limited partner investor with added diversification and the ability to invest smaller amounts into a variety of funds.

Disbursements

The investment by venture funds into investee portfolio companies is called "disbursements". A company will receive capital in one or more rounds of financing. A venture firm may make these disbursements by itself or in many cases will co-invest in a company with other venture firms ("co-investment" or "syndication"). This syndication provides more capital resources for the investee company. Firms co-invest because the company investment is congruent with the investment strategies of various venture firms and each firm will bring some competitive advantage to the investment.

The venture firm will provide capital and management expertise and will usually also take a seat on the board of the company to ensure that the investment has the best chance of being successful. A portfolio company may receive one round, or in many cases, several rounds of venture financing in its life as needed. A venture firm may not invest all of its committed capital, but will reserve some capital for later investment in some of its successful companies with additional capital needs.

Exits

Depending on the investment focus and strategy of the venture firm, it will seek to exit the investment in the portfolio company within three to five years of the initial investment. While the initial public offering may be the most glamourous and heralded type of exit for the venture capitalist and owners of the company, most successful exits of venture investments occur through a merger or acquisition of the company by either the original founders or another company. Again, the expertise of the venture firm in successfully exiting its investment will dictate the success of the exit for themselves and the owner of the company.

IPO

The initial public offering is the most glamourous and visible type of exit for a venture investment. In recent years technology IPOs have been in the limelight during the IPO boom of the last six years. At public offering, the venture firm is considered an insider and will receive stock in the company, but the firm is regulated and restricted in how that stock can be sold or liquidated for several years. Once this stock is freely tradable, usually after about two years, the venture fund will distribute this stock or cash to its limited partner investor who may then manage the public stock as a regular stock holding or may liquidate it upon receipt. Over the last twenty-five years, almost 3000 companies financed by venture funds have gone public.

Mergers and Acquisitions

Mergers and acquisitions represent the most common type of successful exit for venture investments. In the case of a merger or acquisition, the venture firm will receive stock or cash from the acquiring company and the venture investor will distribute the proceeds from the sale to its limited partners.

Valuations

Like a mutual fund, each venture fund has a net asset value, or the value of an investor's holdings in that fund at any given time. However, unlike a mutual fund, this value is not determined through a public market transaction, but through a valuation of the underlying portfolio. Remember, the investment is illiquid and at any point, the partnership may have both private companies and the stock of public companies in its portfolio. These public stocks are usually subject to restrictions for a holding period and are thus subject to a liquidity discount in the portfolio valuation.

Each company is valued at an agreed-upon value between the venture firms when invested in by the venture fund or funds. In subsequent quarters, the venture investor will usually keep this valuation intact until a material event occurs to change the value. Venture investors try to conservatively value their investments using guidelines or standard industry practices and by terms outlined in the prospectus of the fund. The venture investor is usually conservative in the valuation of companies, but it is common to find that early stage funds may have an even more conservative valuation of their companies due to the long lives of their investments when compared to other funds with shorter investment cycles.

Management Fees

As an investment manager, the general partner will typically charge a management fee to cover the costs of managing the committed capital. The management fee will usually be paid ?uarterly for the life of the fund or it may be tapered or curtailed in the later stages of a fund's life. This is most often negotiated with investors upon formation of the fund in the terms and conditions of the investment.

Carried Interest

"Carried interest" is the term used to denote the profit split of proceeds to the general partner. This is the general partners' fee for carrying the management responsibility plus all the liability and for providing the needed expertise to successfully manage the investment. There are as many variations of this profit split both in the size and how it is calculated and accrued as there are firms.

THREE
Venture Capital Company

Venture capital firm have long term plans and they are often ready to take high risks with the intention of earning higher rewards. Apart from being just passive financiers, Venture capitalists assist companies through their active participation. Venture capitalists involve in activities relating to management, strategic marketing and planning of their companies with whom they are investing. They can be called as entrepreneurs first and second as financiers. It is known that venture firms will invest in companies that are in their initial stages of growth. However, venture capitalists also invest in companies that are in various stages of their business life cycle. Venture capitalist may provide capital to a company who may be in the first or second stages of its business development. A venture capitalist will go ahead to invest even before the real product has been launched. It also goes to the extent of providing finance to a company who wants to grow or rather expand its business extensively.

There are many types of venture capital firms and funds organized as a limited partnership entity is common. In this case the venture capital firm serves as the general partner. Having said this, it is the independent venture firm that is considered as the most common type of venture firm and it has no affiliation with regard to other financial institution. You can call these types as "private independent firms". Some venture firms are successful by having a joint venture with those companies which can support each other and grow accordingly. For example: one company has a good technological software product, but lacks in the ability of ac?uiring an ade?uate distribution technology. In such a situation, this company can be paired up with the joint venture company who has better distribution technology. Venture firms are private firms. They cannot exit before the maturity or expiry of the partnership deal.

A venture capital firm can be understood as a private partnership. Venture capital firms are basically providing opportunities for entrepreneurs to flourish. Venture capital firms get finance entrepreneur news with great caution and they are always alert about the rate of return of their venture capital investments. Venture capital is not meant for everyone. It is not meant for all types of entrepreneurs. It is meant for those entrepreneurs who want to make it big in the industry and thus want to join the big leagues. The venture capitalist go through many investment opportunities before investing in only selected companies who show favorable investment opportunities. Venture capitalists may invest in companies dealing with construction, industrial products, business services etc. But there are also other venture capitalists who have specialized investment strategies. For example: a venture capitalist may specialize in retail company investment and there might be another venture capitalist who would prefer to invest in only companies who have just started their business and need financial assistance to grow.

While the terms and conditions of venture capital are not standardized, there are some salient features of venture capital arrangements. The venture capital firm is inclined to assume a high degree of risk in the expectation of earning a high rate of return. The venture capital firm, in addition to providing funds, takes an active interest in guiding the assisted firm. The financial burden for the assisted firm tends to be negligible in the first few years. The venture capital firm normally plans to liquidate its investment in the assisted firm after 3 to 5 years. Typically, the promoter of the assisted firm is given the first option to ac?uire the e?uity investment held by the venture capital firm.

Venture capital firms can raise funds from different sources. The important long-term sources of finance are issue of equity shares and preference shares, issue of debentures of different types, raising of term loans from financial institutions and generation of reserves. Venture capital firms may use different combinations of these sources by considering their relative cost and availability and their impact on the value of the firm. Accordingly, a company can have patterns of capital structure such as e?uity shares only, e?uity shares and preference shares, e?uity shares and debentures, e?uity shares and preference shares reserves, e?uity shares and preference shares debentures, e?uity shares and preference shares/debentures reserves.

The capital structure of venture capital firms is influenced by number of factors such as trading on e?uity, growth and stability of sales. Trading on equity means the use of long-term, fixed interest bearing sources of finance along with e?uity capital. Adopting trading on equity can increase the return on equity. However, this is possible only when the return on investment is more than the cost of finance.

Types of Firms

There are several types of venture capital firms, but most mainstream firms invest their capital through funds organized as limited partnerships in which the venture capital firm serves as the general partner. The most common type of venture firm is an independent venture firm that has no affiliations with any other financial institution. These are called "private independent firms". Venture firms may also be affiliates or subsidiaries of a commercial bank, investment bank or insurance company and make investments on behalf of outside investors or the parent firm's clients. Still other firms may be subsidiaries of non-financial, industrial corporations making investments on behalf of the parent itself. These latter firms are typically called "direct investors" or "corporate venture investors."

Other organizations may include government affiliated investment programs that help start up companies either through state, local or federal programs. One common vehicle is the Small Business Investment Company or SBIC program administered by the Small Business Administration, in which a venture capital firm may augment its own funds with federal funds and leverage its investment in qualified investee companies.

While the predominant form of organization is the limited partnership, in recent years the tax code has allowed the formation of either Limited Liability Partnerships, ("LLPs"), or Limited Liability Companies ("LLCs"), as alternative forms of organization. However, the limited partnership is still the predominant organizational form. The advantages and disadvantages of each has to do with liability, taxation issues and management responsibility.

The venture capital firm will organize its partnership as a pooled fund; that is, a fund made up of the general partner and the investors or limited partners. These funds are typically organized as fixed life partnerships, usually having a life of ten years. Each fund is capitalized by commitments of capital from the limited partners. Once the partnership has reached its target size, the partnership is closed to further investment from new investors or even existing investors so the fund has a fixed capital pool from which to make its investments.

Like a mutual fund company, a venture capital firm may have more than one fund in existence. A venture firm may raise another fund a few years after closing the first fund in order to continue to invest in companies and to provide more opportunities for existing and new investors. It is not uncommon to see a successful firm raise six or seven funds consecutively over the span of ten to fifteen years. Each fund is managed separately and has its own investors or limited partners and its own general partner. These funds' investment strategy may be similar to other funds in the firm. However, the firm may have one fund with a specific focus and another with a different focus and yet another with a broadly diversified portfolio. This depends on the strategy and focus of the venture firm itself.

FOUR

Finding a Venture Capital Company

Many ventures are faced with the challenging task of raising venture capital. The first part of this process is finding the right venture capital firm (VC). While this may seem simple, it isn't. There are thousands of venture capital firms in the United States alone, and going after the wrong ones is one of the most common reasons why companies fail to raise the capital they need.

When seeking a venture capital firm, there are six key variables to consider: location, sector preference, stage preference, partners, portfolio and assets.

Location: most venture capital firms only invest within 100 miles of their office(s). By investing close to home, the firms are able to more actively get involved with and add value to their portfolio companies.

Sector preference: many venture capital firms focus on specific sectors such as healthcare, information technology (IT), wireless technologies, etc. In most cases, even if you have a great company, if you fall outside of the VC's sector preference, they'll pass on the opportunity.

Stage preference: VCs tend to focus on different stages of ventures. For instance, some VCs prefer early stage ventures where the risk is great, but so are the potential returns. Conversely, some VCs focus on providing capital to firms to bridge capital gaps before they go public.

Partners: Venture capital firms are comprised of individual partners. These partners make investment decisions and typically take a seat on each portfolio company's Board. Partners tend to invest in what they know, so finding a partner that has past work experience in your industry is very helpful. This relevant experience allows them to more fully understand your venture's value proposition and gives them confidence that they can add value, thus encouraging them to invest.

Portfolio: Just as you should seek venture capital firms whose partners have experience in your industry, the ideal venture capital firm has portfolio companies in your field as well. Portfolio company management, since they are industry experts, often advises VCs as to whether the company in question is worthwhile. In addition, if your venture has potential synergies with a portfolio company, this significantly enhances the VCs interest in your firm.

Assets: Most companies seeking venture capital for the first time will re?uire subse?uent rounds of capital. As such, it is helpful if the VC has "deep pockets," that is, enough cash to participate in follow-on rounds. This will save the company significant time and effort in maintaining an adequate cash balance.

Finding the right venture capital firm is absolutely critical to companies seeking venture capital. Success results in the capital required and significant assistance in growing your venture. Conversely, failing to find the right firm often results in raising no capital at all and being unable to grow the venture.

FIVE
OBTAINING VENTURE CAPITAL

If you are an inventor or an entrepreneur, obtaining venture capital funding is most likely a major concern for you and your business. During the dot com boom, venture capitalists were fueling the growth, research, and ventures of many new companies. Now that the dot com boom has cooled, those worried about obtaining venture capital for business startup may have a more difficult time securing funding for their budding business.

Venture capital money can come in many different forms. There are companies that specialize in researching new companies to invest in, in order to earn a modest return on their investors money. These companies receive thousands of re?uests for funding monthly and may decide to fund one to two small start-ups a month. Some venture capital companies specialize in specific projects such as real estate or a technology based company. Many large, corporate construction projects are funded via some sort of venture capital agreement.

Another way to obtain venture capital for a business start up is through angel investors. An angel investor can be an individual or a group of investors that gather in order to decide which businesses have the most likely hood of succeeding. Once a business has been selected, the paperwork is drafted for the loan agreement and the business start up is funded by the individual or group angel investors. This method of obtaining venture capital for business startup may also be called hard money or hard money lending.

Recently, obtaining venture capital for business startup has come to reality television. The reality show focused on inventors that had developed a product for introduction to the retail market. The investor was coached and given seed money in order to fully develop their product. This competition played out over several months on reality television with a winner being chosen at the end. The winner was chose based upon how the judges rated the potential retail market success of the inventors product. This reality show was a neat little twist to the venture capital process.

If all of this has you a bit concerned or confused about obtaining venture capital for business startup, there is a bit of good news. The good news is that there is still capital available. If you have a solid business plan or product that you are seeking funding for, your chances are relatively high of getting the funding that you need. Venture capitalists may not be throwing money around like they once were but there is still money available for those that are deemed fit via a solid business plan.

SIX
FINANCING TIPS

Few words carry more fascination to an entrepreneur than "venture capital." The two words may mean different things to different people. Across the world, venture capital means the freedom to have the money to turn your idea from the workbench or the lab into reality.

In short, venture capital is money designed for high-risk investment in startup enterprises. It involves high risk for the investor in beginning ventures or later stages to continue expected progress and growth. It also holds out the possibility of large profits in exchange for the risk of investing.

Venture capital differs from standard bank financing. Instead of paying back a conventional loan within a designated time period at a predetermined rate of interest, venture capital fund investments are repaid through a negotiable percentage of the entrepreneur's stock in the business over three to seven or eight years as the company succeeds and grows. In most cases, a successful initial public offering (IPO) will allow both investor and entrepreneur to prosper by bringing the company's stock to the public market.

Usually, the terms of ownership are negotiated and predetermined before a venture investor will conclude the financing.

How a venture capitalist chooses to structure his investment depends on the style and track record of the venture fund. It can be straight equity, a combination of e?uity and loans, or a sliding scale of reversion from majority control of the entrepreneur's stock to minority ownership upon achievement of certain milestones. Sales and revenues or an anticipated (IPO) are perennial favorites.

The advantages of venture capital for an entrepreneur are quickly apparent. There is usually no re?uirement to repay a bank loan. The venture capitalist and the entrepreneur assume some of the risk of the new business together. Better, there is usually no requirement to tie up funds dedicated to interest. That factor alone can be used to propel the business forward.

Further, the venture capital firm can often bring much needed expertise to a new entrepreneur's business. Beyond capital, knowledgeable and well-connected investors can further lend invaluable knowledge to the startup firm.

Sharing ownership and control of the entrepreneur's business is often considered the chief disadvantage of the involvement of venture capitalists. This is often the main reason for lack of success for small, inexperienced entrepreneurs, resulting in a failed deal.

Before even considering the small, but powerful area of venture capital, the entrepreneur must know and understand two chief areas of concern

- First, the entrepreneur's industry expertise and background should be flawless. It should be on the

cutting edge of industry development.
- The startup company must understand the rigors of successfully running a business, as well as marketing, no matter its industry.
- It should show a third-party perspective to prove the need for its product by the industry or retail consumer.
- Finally, it should clearly demonstrate the fact that the proposed business can grow and achieve profitability in record time.

Secondly, the entrepreneur should consider the most appropriate "fit" with the chosen venture firm. That requires an understanding of the venture firm's preferred emphasis on investment, the expected time frame for funding, its venture partners, successful previous funding and desired geographic locale.

The job of choosing a venture capital source is far from simple.

It runs the gamut from your wealthy cousin who has always liked you and has just inherited a few hundred thousand or millions of dollars. He might be one of a handful of people who know you directly and can serve as "seed capital" funders for you and your enterprise.

Despite a lingering slow-down in the worldwide economy, there is always plenty of money available for the entrepreneur with a well-thought-out novel idea. The only thing re?uired is more attention to research and facts.

SEVEN

Attracting VC

As a startup business in these tough economic times, it can be extremely difficult to make a success of your firm. Any helping hand that you can get is a great help and can be the difference between success and failure. Venture capital is essential, especially if you have an early stage, risk orientated firm - these are the companies that venture capitalists specialize in. However, it is not easy to attain venture capital, as for most companies of this type only around 2 percent of the firms that they look at will even get an interview. An even lower percentage actually receive the investment. For this reason, many startup businesses want to know how to attract venture capital.

As with any type of business plan, preparation is vital. You must be sure to allocate a significant amount of time and man power to attain the funding. If you want a company to take a gamble on you it is absolutely paramount that you have all of your finances in order. If a venture capital company looks at your books and sees discrepancies then you will fall at the first post. If possible, it is good to have a number of personal references in place that can vouch for your reliability and the consumer demand for your products.

When you are looking for any kind of financial investment whether it be from a bank or another company, having a sound business plan and summary is vital. This will be the first impression your potential investor will have of your company, and may impact their decision to proceed further with you. In business, first impressions really do matter.

It is a good idea to look at the various funding processes that the companies you are looking for investment from have. Most have varied approaches, so it is wise to do your research. If possible, speak to other companies that have attained venture capital from them already as they will be able to give you an insight as to what works and what does not. You should also be crystal clear on where the capital will go and what it will be used for to help your business succeed.

It is advisable to have at least 10 different venture capital companies that you want to approach. Once you have sent an individual letter of request to each one, after approximately 2 weeks you should be looking for a personal meeting.

EIGHT

Four Steps

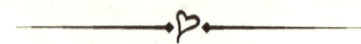

Most startup companies don't have much capital to begin with and struggle to remain open. They turn to outside investor support until they can achieve profitability. If you are the owner of a small business, then you know that getting your company funding is one of the most difficult business challenge you can face.

Seeking this venture capital is an increasingly growing trend fueled by a combination of several factors, such as: improvement in the IPO market, abundant entrepreneurial talent, promising new technologies, and government policies favoring venture capital formation. It's no wonder why venture investors continue to launch and support the development of so many new technologies and business concepts.

Venture capital investments give you and your company the resources it needs to grow to it's full potential since it is used for a variety of things. For example, you can invest in top notch talent, new machinery, manual laborers or you may need to invest in research or new technology. To help put you on the track towards securing venture capital, here are four steps to attract the attention of venture capital investors:

- One of the most important steps is to network. It is one of the first steps in attracting that elusive venture capital. Actually business networking is an important tool for your business all around. The idea behind networking is get the the name of your company out there in the minds of people in the industry and create some buzz around your business idea. If you get the change collect business cards as a way of beginning a path towards contacts.

- You are going to need an experienced team of business partners behind you. One of the things venture capitalists look at it is how well of a structured organization of a company you have and how loyal your co-workers are. Build a diverse team of great minds and sell its credentials to attract some venture capital. TA great group of team members helps to further develop that all crucial buzz which leads to venture capital investment.

- Put together a professional presentation to sell your company's goal and ideas. A smooth, sophisticated presentation should answers all possible ?uestions clearly and avoids any challenges with solutions. This should bring your venture capitalist talks to the next step. Give your solid presentation to as many business associates as you can. Always continue to modify it so that it reaches the level of satisfaction it needs.

- Media coverage brings nothing but benefits. Anytime you can to put yourself on TV or get your name in the newspaper, take it. For example, if your company is in the tech-field or involves the internet, contact review sites and magazines. Writing press releases and submitting them to local newspapers is a great way to catch the eye or a possible venture capital firm.

NINE
HOW TO RISE VC

Venture capitalists see thousands if not tens of thousands of business plans every year. They typically fund fewer than three. To raise money from a VC, you need to set yourself apart from the crowd.

Every venture capitalist is different. While they may all look similar from the perspective of an entrepreneur, speaking as someone who has been on both sides of the table I can tell you that they all have uni?ue and different expectations about what makes a great company.

Some venture capitalists like to follow the herd, that is, they invest in a category that a lot of other investors are making bets in. So if communities are hot and you have a great company idea for a community, and a great team, you may be able to raise money simply because you have a company in a hot space.

Other venture investors take a contrarian approach. They want to fund against the grain. They will invest in enterprise software companies when few other investors are. Or they will fund a company that many other investors have passed on (e.g. declined to invest in).

Venture investors typically (but not always) don't make multiple investments in a single sub-category. Within the large category of Internet startups, for example, a particular firm may already have invested in a company in the sub-category of online shopping. So if you have an online shopping company (to continue the example), it's highly unlikely that a firm that already has a similar investment will invest in you as well. In fact, in general, it's probably unwise to pitch that firm on your idea.

Because venture investors get to make so few investments over the course of their careers, they have to make investments in companies they believe will be big. Not every firm has to make exclusively big investments. Some firms like to diversify by investing in highly risky but potentially big opportunities while also investing in somewhat smaller but less risky companies. But to deliver the sort of returns the investors in the firms expect, most venture investments have to be in big companies. Many pitches present features or products, but not venture fundable companies.

Many of us believe that we have the next multi-million dollar idea that will revolutionize an industry. However, funding is usually the greatest obstacle in order to get a project off the ground. Raising capital is not an easy thing to do in any economy, much less an economy that is struggling. Elevator speeches and fancy poster board presentations will get you as far as the front door of an office, if you're lucky.

The objective of any VC is to financially benefit their investors through your company. They will buy in, filtrate whether or not it is successful, and find an exit strategy. It is important to be fully prepared when using venture capitalists for your business. Here are five basic guidelines to follow when funding through venture capitalists.

1. Its Launch Time

Most all venture capitalists are not looking to buy an idea, but are looking to see how well you have launched your company thus far. If they see you didn't put forth the effort of starting the company, they won't put forth the effort for you in funding the company. Business plans are as useful as a stack of old magazines to investors because no venture capitalist will read one! Spend the time on making your business startup successful rather than behind a computer typing out a 100 page business plan. You do not have to have your company in a fully operational stage, but you should have the ability to show the investors that you have initiated a successful startup for your company. Let the investors know the direction you see the company going in and ask for the funding to allow for your business to continue in that direction.

2. Know the investors

In today's market, most venture capitalists work through large companies, sometimes making it more difficult to find the personal business relationship most people predict they will find. There are different types of investors for the startup phase, expansion phase, and the buyout phase. It is important that you make it clear which type of venture capitalist you need to speak with before you ask for funding. It is hard for any individual to give money to someone they do not know or trust. Do your research before going into any meeting and look up company websites to see what type of companies they have invested in. Ask current companies how their experiences have been through funding with that venture capitalist. Most importantly, when looking for an investor, make sure that you take all information that they have to offer you. They would not be investing if they did not have an idea of where your company can go, so it is important not only because of their financial backing, but their business experience as well.

3. Back to the basics

Once you have started your company and know exactly what type of investor you are looking for, it is time to prepare your presentation to the investors. Make your pitch simple enough that a group of third graders could understand what your business model is. If they can understand, any venture capitalist can as well. Dress to impress and show confidence in your business and the direction you see your business going in the future. Bring along samples or prototypes of your products so the investors can have a hands on experience and get a tangible idea of what your company can offer to them.

Take the time to stop and ask the investors if they understand what your business ideas and ask them if they have any ?uestions. If they do have ?uestions and you do not know the answers, simply say that you do not know. It is very likely that they will have the answers for you, which they can contribute to your business if they do in fact give you their funding. Lastly, make sure they know exactly how much funding you are asking for and what stake in the company they will be receiving for that funding.

4. Don't put all your eggs in one basket.

It is likely that if a venture capitalist likes the business model you have shown, they will try and renegotiate the terms of their stake. It is important for you to be prepared before the fact with a written proposal for each individual. In this folder, you should include any information about your company, bylaws, current financials, and operating agreements. Showing your proposal to each investor will let them know your current thoughts and projections in the company, as well as set a guideline for negotiation. If your product or service is something that is highly sought after with investors, it puts you in control of the situation. If one venture capitalist sees that another investor is interested, it creates competition and will ultimately give your company credibility. Most likely this will make your negotiations favorable to you, driving each investor's stake lower until you reach an agreement that you feel is best for your company.

5. Maintenance

Once your company is funded through a venture capitalist, it is important to maintain a relationship with the investors. Always remember, you may control the company, but the investors can pull the plug on your funding at any time so make them a major part in all decisions and include them in the success of your business. Maintain constant communication and allow access to financial reports to your investors, giving them peace of mind that you are running a successful company. Healthy relationships between companies and investors can lead to future potential expansion with the confident funding to back the projects.

Today's economy is making it more and more difficult to find funding through banks, so many people are going through venture capitalists. Always remember when going through investors, make sure that you are prepared before asking for funding. Know exactly how much your company needs, and how much of your company you are willing to give up. Create competition between investors and always maintain a relationship with any potential venture capitalist that is involved in your company. If you follow these guidelines, using a venture capitalist to fund your ideas will be a smooth transaction.

TEN
ELEMENTS OF A TERM-SHEET

If you have successfully sold your business concept to a venture capitalist, the next step will be the term sheet. This is basically the offer letter stating how much the VC will buy, at what price, and under what terms. Term sheets can be incredibly simple, one to two page documents or incredibly complex and lengthy.

If you receive an incredibly complex and lengthy term-sheet, reconsider that VC as a potential investor. If this is the first document you are getting from them, imagine how complex the actual investor rights and subscription agreements will be. This will mean an expensive legal bill which, by the way, will be sent to you.

Basics of the offer:

Closing date - an estimated date upon which they expect to have the legal work wrapped up and you will receive your money.

Investors - who will be joining the party. You may have more than one venture capital firm invest in your company (especially at later stages).

Amount raised - how much they will be giving you. Price per share - what they plan on paying you per share.

Pre-money valuation - what they deem your company is worth without their money. Capitalization - this is often split into pre- and post-valuation terms. It states how many shares there are outstanding prior to the investment and how many shares will be outstanding after the investment.

Basics of the terms:

Dividends - the stock that the venture capitalist will want will either be preferred or participating-preferred. At some point when your company is successful, the VCs will want to convert their stock to common stock - for sales purposes. They want to make sure that they have the same dividend rights that common stockholders have. In some cases, they want to have dividend rights that the common stockholders don't have (nice, huh?). This will also be listed here - try to negotiate away from cumulative dividends as this is an unpaid dividend that accumulates to the preferred shareholder and is payable upon li?uidation or redemption. It's a way to give a higher valuation to you feel good, but actually get more of your company without putting in any more money.

Li?uidation preference - This is what happens when you either (1) liquidate the company or (2) sell it/IPO. In general, you would think that the VC owns 40% of your company, they would get 40% of the profit. Well, if they have straight preferred, this is true, but they have come up with a special construct to make sure they get a little bit more: participating preferred. See the example below for an explanation.

Liquidation Preference Example:

In the old days, VCs would invest $5 million in a company worth $5 million pre-investment and get 50% of the company of preferred shares.

At the time of sale, the VCs would get money back in this way:

1. Sale price: $7 million. VC's get their $5 million back, the founders get $2 million. (This is the preferred part - they get their money back before the common shareholders get a payout.)

2. Sale price: $10 million. VCs convert to common and the VCs get half and the founders get half (each $5 million).

In this case the company has to be sold for over $10 million for the VCs to make any return.

In the days of the internet boom... VCs realized they were throwing their money behind some pretty crappy stuff, thus some clever MBA financial engineer introduced the participating preferred shares. Same example: VCs invest $5 million in a company worth $5 million pre-investment and get 50% of the company of preferred shares. However, the participating part means they get their money back before the rest is split up according to ownership.

1. Sale price: $7 million. VC's get their $5 million back, then the founders and the VCs split the remaining $2 million 50/50. In this case, founders get $1 million.

2. Sale price: $10 million. VC's get their $5 million back, then the founders and the VCs split the remaining $5 million 50/50. Founders get $2.5 million.

In this case the company has to be sold for over $5 million for the VCs to make any return - a much lower hurdle.

The multiplier part is the amount the VCs want to get back before any gets split between the shareholders. In the above case, if the investment was 1.5x participating return, the VCs would re?uire $7.5 million be paid to them first, then the remaining amount would be split between the VCs and the founders.

Voting rights - this lays out how the VC is allowed to vote his shares. Usually, they set it up so that even if they have a minority share, they have the majority of the votes when it comes to anything important ("protective provisions").

Protective Provisions - the VC wants to make sure that they can protect their investment. They will want the right to be able to say whether they sell the company or not, whether there is any conversion to common, add board members, borrow money, etc.

Anti-dilution Provisions - another tool for the VC to protect his investment. Let's say the VC owns 40% worth $4M and you own 60% worth $6M. You need to raise more money ($4M), but you can only find a pre-money valuation of $8M. If dilution was allowed, the end result would be VC2 gets 33.3%, your share would be reduced to 40%, VC1's share would be reduced to 26.6%. If anti-dilution provisions are in place, the end result would be VC2 gets 33.3%, your share would be reduced to 26.6%, VC1's share would stay at 40%. Ouch.

Redemption Rights - what happens if your company becomes one of the living dead. If you build a decent company and you're making a nice living, but the company is not growing at a rate that will attract a buyer or make possible an IPO, the VC is eventually going to want his money back. This gives them the right to get it back (plus any dividends accrued). This usually kicks in after the fifth year and is payable over a few years.

Representations and Warrantees - the escape clause. They will say that you have represented certain things to them, such as revenue growth, customers, etc. After you have signed the term sheet, they will comb through your books and records and if they don't like what they see, they will back out.

Conditions to closing - another escape clause. This should note that the offer is made predicated on beliefs that may change after they look after you books. It also contains some legalese about meeting appropriate filing and legal re?uirements.

This pretty much covers the basics of the easy term-sheet. A more extensive term-sheet is likely to contain the investor rights terms which continues on in the protective vein, making sure that the VC has the first shot of their shares being sold if the company goes public, that the company (not the VC) pays for the registration of shares, what sort of information rights the VC has, whether the VC has the right to participate in future rounds, what re?uires investor approval, and any re?uired non-disclosure and non-compete provisions.

The term-sheet will also most likely contain an expiration date and a no-shop provision to ensure that you are unable to find another term-sheet to have as a comparison. You goal in this case is to have several potential investors who all give you term-sheets at the same time.

Your job is to negotiate your deal to your best advantage. Do not spend too much time worrying about the valuation, but instead pay attention to the control provisions and negotiate those.

ELEVEN

Rejecting Reasons

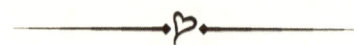

Do not be frustrated if you have failed to raise capital from venture capital funds. Only a very small percentage of companies do raise capital from venture capital funds - and in the current environment, this percentage is even less.

Main Reasons rejected by venture capital funds

- The deal is too small - many venture capital funds have mandates - minimum investment would be $1 million or $10m, if you are just seeking for a small capital, they will not talk to you.

- New Company - start-ups should go for alternatives rather than venture capital funds, there are specific start-up funding providers or investors or apply for grants.

- Lack of existing revenue - Look, let us be realistic about it - would you invest in a business that has no revenue established or a business that has 3 years of revenue. If you have made profit, even a small profit, show venture capital companies that. Some have said that it is 10 times harder for a business to raise capital without revenue.

- Too Technical - You have the best idea but unable to express them in plain English (or other languages) to venture capital firms. Remember what Warren Buffet's golden rule - "Never invest in things you do not understand"

- Relying on Corporate Advisors and Brokers - If you do nothing and rely on corporate advisors or brokers, it will be impossible to raise capital. You have to work with them closely, you have to improve your business, write press releases, advisors or brokers can not do them for you.

- Demonstrate that "I do not need the money" - ironically, venture capital funds always like to invest in businesses that are already sustainable or already on track - the businesses that actually do not capital to survive but the capital to grow or expand. If you can demonstrate that, venture capital funds will come and knock on your door.

So, rule no.1 is always build up your business first, make it worthwhile then talk to venture capital funds - not raise the capital first and build the business.

Unless your ideas or applications are really state-of-art, and there is no shortage of great concepts that have raised money from venture capital such as MySpace, Twitters or eve Facebook - but all of them have demonstrated there is a solid business- such as number of members, members growth rate - these are also regarded as company assets.

Remember, Hotmail was sold to Microsoft - because it has millions of registered users - and smart companies can use them for marketing purpose. So, when comes to asset of the company, sometimes it is not just the financial aspects, but what your company can really bring and that is your special point.

Disclaimer

Introduction

By using this book, you accept this disclaimer in full.

No advice

The book contains information. The information is not advice and should not be treated as such.

No representations or warranties

To the maximum extent permitted by applicable law and subject to section below, we exclude all representations, warranties, undertakings and guarantees relating to the book.

Without prejudice to the generality of the foregoing paragraph, we do not represent, warrant, undertake or guarantee:

- that the information in the book is correct, accurate, complete or non-misleading.

- that the use of the guidance in the book will lead to any particular outcome or result.

Limitations and exclusions of liability

The limitations and exclusions of liability set out in this section and elsewhere in this disclaimer: are subject to section 6 below; and govern all liabilities arising under the disclaimer or in relation to the book, including liabilities arising in contract, in tort (including negligence) and for breach of statutory duty.

We will not be liable to you in respect of any losses arising out of any event or events beyond our reasonable control.

We will not be liable to you in respect of any business losses, including without limitation loss of or damage to profits, income, revenue, use, production, anticipated savings, business, contracts, commercial opportunities or goodwill.

We will not be liable to you in respect of any loss or corruption of any data, database or software.

We will not be liable to you in respect of any special, indirect or consequential loss or damage.

Exceptions

Nothing in this disclaimer shall: limit or exclude our liability for death or personal injury resulting from negligence; limit or exclude our liability for fraud or fraudulent misrepresentation; limit any of our liabilities in any way that is not permitted under applicable law; or exclude any of our liabilities that may not be excluded under applicable law.

Severability

If a section of this disclaimer is determined by any court or other competent authority to be unlawful and/or unenforceable, the other sections of this disclaimer continue in effect.

If any unlawful and/or unenforceable section would be lawful or enforceable if part of it were deleted, that part will be deemed to be deleted, and the rest of the section will continue in effect.

Law and jurisdiction

This disclaimer will be governed by and construed in accordance with Swiss law, and any disputes relating to this disclaimer will be subject to the exclusive jurisdiction of the courts of Switzerland.

www.ingramcontent.com/pod-product-compliance
Lightning Source LLC
Chambersburg PA
CBHW020711180526
45163CB00008B/3035